MOVE

 how to fulfill
God's will
for your life

daniel king

Special Thanks to Our Friends Who Made this Edition Possible:

Joshua Atkinson, Pastors Michael & Darlene Bowen - Wings as Eagles Church, Elmer & Monta Lynn Brown, Cindy L. Douglas, Drs. Mike & Kristina Earls, Sonia & Chelsea Gould, Dorla Gregory, Merritt & Meggin Hunt, Justin James, Pastor Carole Lowe - Liberty Church, Don & Brenda Perry, Abner Herico Rosales, Pastors Isaias & Joyce Sanchez - Lord of the Harvest Church, Pastor Hendrik A. Sarioa - Bethany Assembly of God Church, May Ling Shen, Edisha Putra Sinulingga, Bethany Spaulding, Joshua Wagner, Debra Young

All rights reserved under International Copyright Law. Contents and/or cover may not be reproduced in whole or in part in any form without the express written consent of the author.

Move: How to Fulfill God's Will for Your Life

ISBN: 1-931810-08-7

Copyright: 2010
Daniel King
King Ministries International
PO Box 701113
Tulsa, OK 74170 USA

1-877-431-4276

daniel@kingministries.com

www.kingministries.com

Table of Contents

Introduction
Chapter 1 - What is God's Will for Your Life?   7
Chapter 2 - God's Word is God's Will   11
Chapter 3 - Be Still or Do His Will?   15
Chapter 4 - Is God's Will a Dot or a Circle?   21
Chapter 5 - Does God Give Us a Map or a Compass?   25
Chapter 6 - Get Your "But" Out of My Way   29
Chapter 7 - God Celebrates Your Choices   33
Chapter 8 - Who Controls Your Destiny?   37
Chapter 9 - Are you a Saul or a Jonathan?   43
Chapter 10 - Does God Guide Your Sitting?   49
Chapter 11 - Backwards? Stay Frozen? Move Forwards?   55
Chapter 12 - Your Success is Motion-Activated   59
Chapter 13 - Movement Activates the Power of Prayer   63
Chapter 14 - A Word from God for Your Life   67
Chapter 15 - Are You Waiting on God?   73
Chapter 16 - How Can You Discover God's Will?   77
Chapter 17 - Steps to Fulfill Your Destiny   85
Epilogue

I challenge you to get up and start moving toward your destiny.

Introduction

What is God's will for your life? What do you plan to accomplish with your time here on earth? Do you ever wonder about the next step God wants you to take?

In this book you will learn the secret to finding and fulfilling God's will for your life. The key is to move.

Many believers are confused about how to find God's will for their lives. I know people who sit and wait for years because they are too frightened to move without clear direction. They are paralyzed by indecision and never take the first step toward fulfilling their destiny.

Another group of Christians take action and move aggressively toward their destiny. Sometimes these believers make mistakes, but when they fall, they quickly pick themselves back up and keep moving. Ultimately this second group of "movers" accomplish far more than the first group of people who sit around waiting for instructions.

To which group do you belong? I want to motivate you to stop sitting still while asking "What does God want me to do?" and to challenge you to get up and start moving toward your destiny.

In this book you will meet my friend Zachary. We recently had some conversations that changed him from a "sitter" into a "mover" and helped him begin to fulfill his destiny. I pray that God speaks to your heart as you hear his story.

Moving with God,

Daniel King

How can I discover
God's will for my life?

chapter 1
What is God's Will for Your Life?

I had just purchased a mocha frappuccino when Zach came up behind me. "Daniel, I am really confused," he said with frustration.

"Sit down. I have a few minutes. What's going on?"

He began to passionately tell me all the amazing things he wanted to do for God. Then he poured his heart out, "I have been out of school for five years and none of the dreams that God gave me have come to pass. I have been praying and dreaming, and then praying some more, but nothing seems to work."

Then with a tear in the corner of his eye he made the lament that started me on the journey to writing this book. "Daniel, I don't know what God wants me to do."

As I started to think about his question, my mind drifted back over our history together.

My friend Zachary is a wonderful believer. He loves God with all his heart. He reads his Bible and prays every morning and evening. He goes to church every Sunday morning and sometimes on Wednesday nights. He wears Christian tee-shirts, listens to Christian music, and never goes to R-rated movies.

I met Zach when I was attending Oral Roberts University in Tulsa, Oklahoma. We had a few classes together. Zach has a great sense of humor and I quickly discovered that it was fun to hang out with him. We often met and enjoyed talking about theology. I was always impressed with his smart ideas and his passion for God.

Zach had big dreams. He planned to go to Africa and start a ministry to feed the poor. He wanted to open a Bible school, plant churches, and even start an orphanage. He was always talking about the amazing feats he would do for the kingdom of God.

After we graduated, we did not see each other very often. I would run into him from time to time at a nearby coffee shop. We always had a friendly conversation.

"Hey Zach, how are you doing?" I would ask.

"I'm blessed," he would reply. Then he would usually add something like this, "I'm really praying about what God wants me to do." Then he would launch into a long list of the decisions he was trying to make with God's help.

"I am trying to decide if I should go on a mission trip," he said one time.

Another day he said, "I met a girl that I think is really cute. But I'm not sure if I should ask her out. I'm still praying."

"Lord willing, I am going to start interning with a ministry here in town," he explained one day.

A couple of months later I saw him again. "Did you ever start working with that ministry?" I asked.

"No," he replied, "I almost filled out their application, but I was not sure if it was God's will for me to work with them or not."

I remembered his dream of being a missionary in Africa. I queried him, "Do you want to go with me to Ethiopia? I am doing a big crusade there next month." He said he would pray about coming, but he never did come on that trip or on any of the others I invited him on.

Over a period of about five years, Zach and I had many of these conversations. He was always praying about his next big plan, but I don't recall him ever telling me about something he was actually doing for God.

But on this day, our relationship moved to a deeper level. Over the next few months, it would be absolutely amazing to see what God did in Zach's life.

I rephrased Zach's lament, "So, you want to know what God's will is for your life?"

"Yeah, how can I discover God's will for my life?" Zach asked.

There are two kinds of Christians: the sitters and the movers.

chapter 2
God's Word is God's Will

At first, I did not know how to answer his question. I have always known what God wants me to do. When I was five years old, a prophetess came to my father's church and prophesied that I am called to be an international evangelist. I leaped right into my calling and preached my first sermon at the age of six. My parents became missionaries in Mexico when I was ten and since they were my legal guardians, I had to go with them.

I remember driving through the streets of Mexico with my father. Whenever we saw an empty soccer field, I would pull his sleeve and point at the field, "Dad, we could fill that field up with people and preach to them!" I enjoyed reading books by evangelists T.L. Osborn and Billy Graham. Day and night I would dream about reaching masses of people with the Gospel.

When I was fifteen years old, I read a book about how to be successful. It recommended writing down your goals. The book said that young people should set a goal of becoming a millionaire before the age of thirty. Because of my upbringing as a missionary in Mexico, I realized that money was not important to me; what was important was souls. So I wrote down this goal, "I, Daniel King, want to lead 1,000,000 people to Jesus before I turn thirty." Instead of trying to become a millionaire, I decided to lead a million "heirs" into the kingdom of God.

Immediately I began taking steps toward making the dream come true. I read books about evangelism. I studied the lives of great evangelists and raised money to travel overseas to participate in their crusades. I looked for opportunities to preach and God began to open doors.

Two years before the deadline, I completed my initial goal. Now my wife Jessica and I have set a new goal. We want to lead 1,000,000 people to Jesus every year.

But, Zach's calling is different than my calling. Each individual is unique and God's plan for his life is not the same as God's plan for my life.

I decided to start by asking him about his understanding of how to discover God's will.

Zach gave me the classic textbook answer, "God's Word reveals God's will."

I agreed with him. "God's will for your life is hidden within the pages of His Word. If you obey God's Word, you will be fulfilling His will for your life. It is never God's will for us to do something contrary to His Word. If your course of action is against God's Word, then it is against God's will for your life."

Zach named some verses that reveal God's will. "According to the Ten Commandments in Exodus 20, lying, killing, and committing adultery are clearly outside of God's will. Obviously, if you do any of these things, you are outside of God's will."

I agreed again. "Nothing that is against God's Word can ever be God's will. Period. The simplest way to discover God's will is to ask, "What does God's Word tell me to do?"

He interrupted me. "I understand the Bible reveals God's will, but how do I know what God wants me to do today? I know I should not sin, but how do I know how to choose which mission trip I should go on?"

I continued, "As you obey the general will of God for your life as revealed in the Bible, you will discover the specific will of God for your life. You will never discover God's hidden will for your life until you first do God's known will. God's Word is the beginning point for knowing God's will. Usually those who do not obey His Word find it difficult to hear His voice."

As I talked to Zach, I discovered that he was so paralyzed by fear of missing God's will, that even simple decisions became difficult for him to make. "How do I know if I should go to the grocery store first or fill up my gas tank?" Zach asked. "What do I do when God's Word does not specifically address my current situation? After all, there is no commandment that says, 'Zach, thou shalt marry Michelle.' So, how am I supposed to know whether I should marry my girlfriend Michelle?"

I replied, "Within the confines of God's Word, God gives us great freedom. The Bible reveals God's moral will but in relation to the area of volitional will (our personal choices) we are allowed freedom of choice. Zach, I think you are confused about how to find God's will for your life because you are confused about the choices that God gives us. I have a lot more to say about how to discover God's will for your life, but I am out of time today. Would you like to hang out again on Tuesday?"

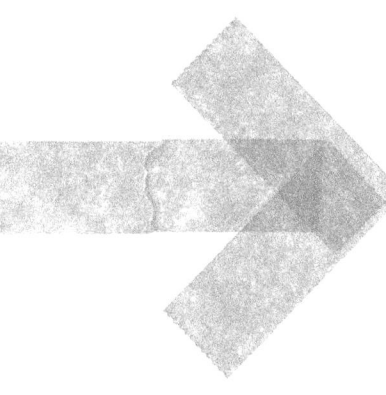

chapter 3
Be Still or
Do His Will?

On Tuesday, Zach and I decided to go for a walk around the local park. We both needed the exercise and it was a beautiful sunny day. The birds were chirping and families were picnicking on the grass. The three-mile trail would give us plenty of time to talk.

I jumped right in, "I think there are two kinds of Christians: the sitters and the movers." I did not tell Zach which kind of Christian I thought he was.

"Let's talk about 'The Sitters' first. Their motto is, 'I do not move without God's guidance.' Those who hold to this philosophy wait and pray until God shows a way. They rarely move without a clear sign or instruction from God. Those who follow this viewpoint sound very holy and proper. They often say things like, 'I am waiting on God. I am trusting God to take care of me. I do not want to miss God and go in the wrong direction. I have faith that God will provide.' Year after year, they sit in the same place, doing the same thing, hoping and praying for God to move." I wondered if Zach recognized some of his own words in my example.

"I call the second group of people, 'The Movers.' They live their lives by a different mantra. If they had to put it into words they would say, 'I expect God's guidance when I move.' They do not sit around waiting for a word from God; instead they begin obeying the commands God has already given them. They expect to receive guidance while they are in the process of moving."

I began to share some of the differences between sitters and movers:

1. Sitters sit; movers move.
2. Sitters listen to God's voice; movers obey God's voice.
3. Sitters are quickly overtaken by movers.
4. Sitters talk about doing great things for God; movers actually do great things for God.
5. Sitters are still asking, "What should we do?" when movers announce, "Look at what we have done."
6. Sitters critique and complain; movers are too busy to attack others.
7. Sitters point out problems; movers fix problems.
8. Sitters say, "I am trusting God." Movers say, "God is trusting me."

I gave Zach an example from my own life. "Several years ago, I asked a pastor if we could hold a special series of evangelistic meetings in his church. He said, 'Let me pray about it.' Now years later, he is still praying about it and wondering why his church has not grown."

"Let me guess," Zach said, "He is a sitter?"

"That's right." I continued, "I held a meeting with another

pastor and six new families started coming to his church. The next year we held another evangelistic outreach and again his church grew. What was the difference between these pastors? While one was praying, the other was doing. One pastor prayed, 'God save the lost.' The second pastor was giving away hotdogs to people in the park on a Saturday morning and demonstrating the love of Christ in a tangible way. The second pastor is a mover. As he takes action, he trusts God to bless his actions."

Then Zach made a really good point. "What about the story of Mary and Martha in Luke 10? Martha was stressed running around and preparing food for Jesus. Mary was sitting at the feet of Jesus spending time with Him. Martha was upset and asked Jesus to make Mary help in the kitchen. Instead, Jesus rebuked Martha and complimented Mary. Doesn't Jesus speak more highly of the sitter in this story than the mover?"

"Let me answer your question with some questions of my own. Does God want us to be still or to do His will? Does God want us to stay still waiting for His presence, or does God want us to take His power to the world? It is true that there is a time and a place for soaking in the presence of God. But while we are soaking, we must not forget that Jesus gave us a job to complete here on earth. Right before Jesus ascended to heaven, He told His disciples to go to the upper room and wait for the gift of the Holy Spirit. On the day of Pentecost, they were all filled with power from the Holy Spirit. Until they were filled, they waited. After they were filled, the wait was over and it was time for them to go. As one preacher said, 'Until you are filled, don't go; after you are filled, don't stay.'

Often people make spiritual excuses for sitting still. They say,

'I'm waiting on the Lord' or 'I don't go because I am waiting for the Lord to reveal His will.' Reinhard Bonnke says, 'Ever since the day of Pentecost, we never again wait for the Lord, the Lord waits for us.'

I'm not saying we should not pray. Even Jesus went off by Himself every day to speak with His Father. However, we should pray as we move instead of using prayer as an excuse for not moving. Oswald Chambers said, 'See that you do not use the trick of prayer to cover up what you know you ought to do.' Our praying, our listening to God, and our moving is a continuous process. As we move, we pray, then listen to God, then move again. It looks like this..."

I knelt down in the dirt and drew a quick diagram.

"In the story of Mary and Martha, Martha was rebuked for being too busy to sit at the feet of Jesus. Because of this, some people have taught that it is much better to sit in the presence of Jesus then it is to be busy doing the work of the ministry. This mentality has paralyzed some Christians and prevented them from taking action. Some people are seventy or eighty years old, still seeking the will of God. They have not accomplished much of anything.

Another story in Mark 5 teaches the opposite lesson. After Jesus cured the demon-possessed man, he begged Jesus for the opportunity to follow Him and sit at His feet. However, Jesus did not permit him, but instead commanded the man to go tell all his friends about his miracle. So, the man departed and proclaimed in the area of Decapolis all that Jesus had done for him.

The word 'Decapolis' means 'ten cities.' The man who had been demon-possessed traveled from city to city, telling people about Jesus. Later in Mark 7:31 when Jesus visited this region, He was able to perform great miracles because the faith of the people had been prepared by the testimony of the man who was set free from demons."

Zach listened to me patiently as I preached a mini-sermon to him, but then he brought up another verse, "What about Psalm 46:10 which says *'Be still and know that I am God?'*"

I smiled because I had a good answer to his question. "Did you ever read the second half of that verse?" I asked.

"Probably, but I can't remember what it says," he admitted.

"It says, *'I will be exalted among the nations. I will be exalted in the earth.'* How will God be exalted among the nations unless we take action and go proclaim His glory in all the nations of the earth? There is a place for sitting at the feet of Jesus and for being still in His presence, but the purpose for this time is to prepare us for taking action!"

As we arrived back at our cars, I left Zach with a joke I heard once from a comedian, "There are three types of people in the world. Those who make things happen, those who watch things happen, and those who wonder, 'What just happened?'"

I finished by challenging him, "I do not want to sit around waiting for things to happen, I want to make them happen. What kind of person do you want to be?"

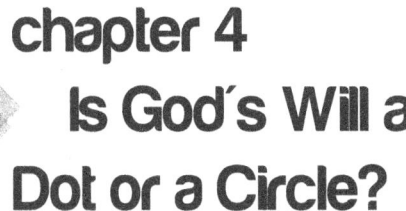

chapter 4
Is God's Will a Dot or a Circle?

Later that week I found some notes on my laptop that I had written about the will of God. I sent it to Zach as an e-mail.

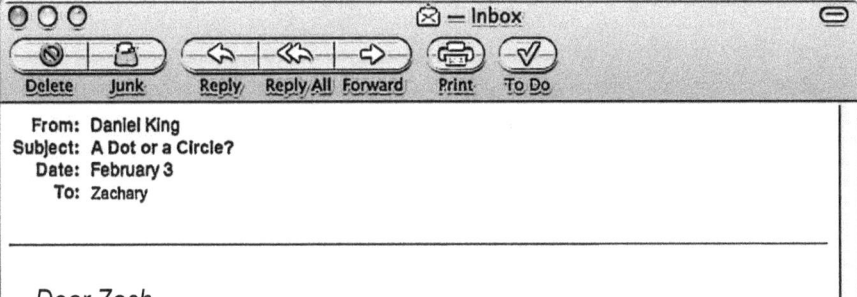

From: Daniel King
Subject: A Dot or a Circle?
Date: February 3
To: Zachary

Dear Zach,

Hi! I had fun chatting and spending time with you in the park. Here are some notes I found on the will of God. Enjoy!

There is a general will of God and a specific will of God. The general will of God is like a circle. The specific will of God is like a small dot within that circle. The Bible reveals the general will of God; our actions help us find the specific will of God for our lives. The difference between the general and the specific aspects of God's will has produced two different theories as to how we should go about discovering God's will.

The "Dot" theory believes that in every case there is one specific action God wants us to take. One person we are supposed to marry. One place we are supposed to go to college. One mission trip we must go on. One color of socks God wants us to wear today. People who always wait for the "dot" to be revealed are usually "sitters."

The "Circle" theory believes there are a variety of actions that please God. There are boundaries (revealed by God's written Word) but within that circle there are a variety of choices that God celebrates. For example, the Bible says we should not marry unbelievers (2 Corinthians 6:14) but within the circle of potential spouses who are born-again and love God there might be many who would please both God and you. People who are willing to make choices within the circle of God's will are usually "movers."

New believers are often "dot" Christians. When my youngest brother was ten years old, I had to tell him, "David, don't run out onto the street." He needed very specific instructions. But now that he is in college, I don't worry about him chasing after cars. Why? Because I can trust him to make wise decisions.

A baby must be told not to touch a hot stove, but an adult knows better. Similarly, a baby believer often needs specific instructions about how to live the Christian life. A mature Christian generally does not need detailed instructions because they have learned enough about the character and nature of God to know what is right and wrong.

Mature Christians have learned to follow the advice of St. Augustine who said, "Love God and do as you please." If you really love God, you want to do what pleases Him. As my friend, Greg Fraser paraphrased, "Love God with all your heart and do whatever else you want." As long as you are in the "circle" of what God wants, there are many choices within that circle that please God equally. When we are within the general will of God, we have great freedom with our specific actions.

Author Randy Alcorn wrote, "The will of God is not wrapped up in the details of what we do, but the character of who we are. It is not just the large choices, but the daily small choices that cumulatively build us into who God wants (wills) us to be. God cares about the little things and His will can include details, but these are secondary. What is primary is that we choose to follow His clear direction in spiritual and moral arenas. Then all the details fall into place from there."

As you walk in the general will of God, you will discover the specific will of God for your life. The way the specific will of God is revealed is through your actions. As you move, God is able to guide you to the specific point He wants you at.

Some think being in God's will is like walking across a tightly-strung tightrope over a deep crevasse. They start at one end of the rope and gingerly take tiny balanced steps until they reach the other side. Even a slight deviation to the right or left can lead to a nasty plunge as they cautiously proceed step-by-step across the rope.

But, I think that being in God's will is more like being a player on a football field. The ultimate goal is to get the football into the end zone on the other side of the field. There are many different plays and ways of getting the ball there. Some run the ball, other players pass the ball, and some kick a field goal. All these methods of getting the ball to the other end of the field make the coach happy, as long as the goal is achieved. There are many paths and many plays that get you to where you need to be.

God the Father has put us on a winning team and given us the best equipment and training. His Playbook is full of winning strategies, and He sits in His skybox cheering us on. The angels and saints are in the stands cheering at the top of their lungs. The opposing team is weak and puny. Our star quarterback, Jesus, has already defeated them. After soundly trouncing the opposition, Jesus was pulled out of the game to go sit next the team owner. Now it is our turn to play. The score is ten thousands points ahead in our favor and we are just playing out the clock.

You and I are not walking a narrow tightrope of faith where disaster looms with each tiny misstep. The tightrope is like the dot; it represents only one pathway to our destiny.

Instead, we are on a wide football field running plays. Our Coach, the Holy Spirit, is calling out encouragement. We are calling audibles, picking our plays as we go. If one play fails, we just get up and try another. Our team has permanent possession of the ball. The field represents the circle of God's will. As long as we stay in the game and do not leave the field, then our heavenly Coach is happy with us.

God Bless,

Daniel King

chapter 5
Does God Give Us a Map or a Compass?

Zach and I met again at the coffee shop a week later. After we both got our drinks, he jumped right in with a question. "How do I get to my destiny? I am waiting for God to map out my life for me."

I thought for a moment. "Zach, I think you are asking the wrong question. Waiting for God to give you a detailed map for your entire life is unrealistic. A road map contains specific directions to a specific destination. If we sit around asking for God to give us a map we will wait around for years. God is more likely to give us a compass heading to follow rather than a map.

"A compass?"

"Each of us is given an inner compass which reveals God's will for our lives. The direction this inner compass is pointing is revealed by our innate talents, interests and gifts. Your strengths and dominant focus reveal your calling. For example, if a teenage girl enjoys spending time with children, this is an indication she might be called to be a teacher, a mother, or a children's minister. Or, if you are always thinking about how to make money, you might be called to be an entrepreneur or businessman. I always had a passion for the lost and was successful at public speaking so this was a good indication that when I decided to become an evangelist, I was headed in the right direction. If I tried to become a worship leader, I would fail because I have no musical talent. Recognizing this fact saves me the trouble of wondering if God has called me to be a music leader."

"That makes sense," Zach said, "I seem to remember that when God called Abraham, God did not give him detailed instructions; instead God just said to leave the city of Ur. God promised to show him his ultimate destination on the way. God gave Abraham the first step, but not the full picture of where he was going. God does not tell us what to do until we begin to move. However, if we start to move we will hear the next step, and then the next, and so on. How does this help me find God's will for my life?"

"In order to discover God's plan for your life, do not sit in a locked room praying until you have a complete vision of where you are going. Start moving in the direction of your greatest interest. Once you start to move, God will guide your steps. God is drawn to movement. Let's look at what the Bible says."

I flipped open my black leather Bible and found Psalm 37:23, *"The steps of a good man are ordered by the Lord, and He delighteth in his way."*

I looked up at Zach, "Notice it says, 'The steps of a good man are ordered.' Once we start taking steps, God is able to show us where to go. God cannot order our steps if we are standing still. You drive and God gives directions, but there are no directions until you start driving. A parked car never goes anywhere even if it is on the right road. Will Rogers said, 'Even if you are on the right track, you'll get run over if you just sit there.' Reinhard Bonnke says, 'People who forever SEEK the will of God are overrun by those who DO the will of God!' In other words, do not wait for A-Z to be revealed. Step out with A-B and God will reveal B-Z as you move."

Does God give us a map or a compass?

You don't drown by falling into water;
you drown by staying there.

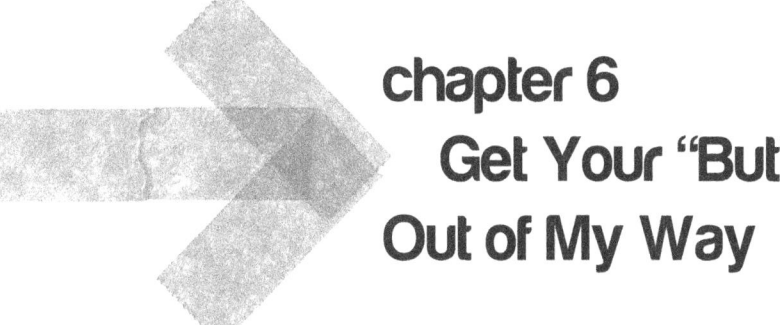

chapter 6
Get Your "But" Out of My Way

Our conversation was interrupted as the girl behind the counter called our names, "Zach. Daniel." Our drinks were ready. As Zach jumped up to grab the steaming coffee mugs, I read the verse again, *"The steps of a good man are ordered by the Lord."*

When Zach sat down, he took me by surprise. Within the next five minutes, he made four excuses (four big "buts") for why he had not started moving toward fulfilling God's plan for his life.

"I want to fulfill God's plan for my life…" he started.

"But?" I queried.

"But, what if I try to do something for God and I fail?" Zach asked.

Immediately, my eyes fell on the very next verse, Psalm 37:24, *"Though he fall, he shall not be utterly cast down: for the Lord upholdeth him with his hand."*

I read the verse out loud, then said, "Notice that it does not say we will never fall. What it does say is that if we fall, God will pick us back up. Falling is never a period on the end of our sentence, only a comma. You wonder, 'But what if I make the wrong choice and head in the wrong direction?' The Bible promises, *'We know that all things work together for good to them that love God who are called according to His purpose'* (Romans 8:28). Even if you make the wrong choice, God will turn it into something good, because He is a good God."

We discussed how failure is not necessarily an indication you are out of God's will. Thomas Edison failed over ten thousand times when he was inventing the electric light bulb. When asked why he kept trying after so many failures he replied, 'I knew I would eventually run out of ways it would not work.' Some fail once and think they are outside God's will, but sometimes we need to keep trying until we succeed.

I continued, "If you fall down, get back up. You don't drown by falling into water; you drown by staying there. Because we live in an imperfect world, bad things can still happen even when we are in the center of God's will for our lives. But God will cause good to come from negative situations.

When Paul was thrown into prison, God used him to minister to the prison guards. He said *'...I want you to know, brethren, that the things which happened to me have actually turned out for the furtherance of the gospel...'* (Philippians 1:12 NKJV).

When his own brothers sold Joseph as a slave into Egypt, God used him to save his whole family during a time of famine. Joseph explained, *'You intended to harm me, but God intended it for good to accomplish what is now being done, the saving of many lives'* (Genesis 50:20 NIV)."

Then Zach mentioned his second excuse for not fulfilling God's will, "But, I'm afraid of what people will think about me."

"There is a huge anonymous group out there named 'They.' And 'They' say all kinds of things. 'They' say you can't wear certain colors together. 'They' say you have to do things a certain way. 'They' say your dream is impossible. 'They' are usually wrong. Satan often uses the fear of man, fear of being rejected by this group called 'They' to stop you from completing your destiny. Stand strong in the Lord, and don't let 'They' run your life."

Zach continued to complain, "But, what if I'm not pleasing God because of my imperfections? Sometimes I just get things wrong."

I sipped my drink and answered, "You are not where you need to be, but thank God you are not where you used to be. Zach, if you were perfect, you would not need a Savior. God is not surprised at your mistakes and imperfections. He knows everything; your faults don't faze Him. I'm not perfect either. I have made mistakes, been distracted, and lost my focus at times; but God still loves me and chooses to use me."

"But, I'm afraid I'll make a wrong decision," Zach said.

"Self-doubt is a weapon from the pit of hell. Be bold! Make decisions. When you decide not to decide, you've made a decision at that moment. It is better to move and be wrong than to never move at all. God would rather have an imperfect performance than a perfect heart that never moves. Often we are so scared we will get it wrong, that we do nothing. You can be sure that while we are doing nothing, the devil is doing something."

We finished our coffee time by praying together that God would help Zach overcome all the excuses that were keeping him from fulfilling his destiny.

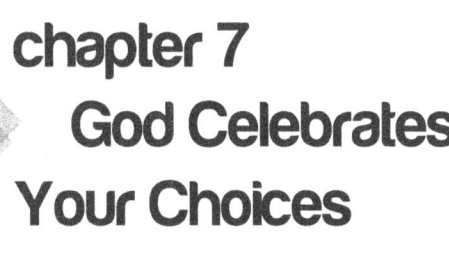

chapter 7
God Celebrates Your Choices

A week later, I sent out a tweet from my cell phone. It said, "God celebrates your choices." Twitter automatically changed my Facebook status. Zach noticed my status update and typed a comment, "What do you mean?"

The next day we got together again to talk about it. Whether he liked it or not, Zach was in for another long talk. That's the thing about being a preacher, when someone asks me a question I tend to answer with a sermon.

I began, "God celebrates your choices. God gave Adam and Eve a great gift. It was the gift of free choice. We are not robots. We have the ability to make our own choices. God is excited to go along with many of our choices. The good God has planned for you is not limited by one choice. Your wrong or imperfect choices can still produce good outcomes because according to Romans 8:28, God works all things together for our good.

You were not born to make right or wrong decisions. You were created to make decisions, then to make those decisions the right ones. God gave us dominion on this earth. When we take dominion, God backs our choices, as long as those choices are within God's will as revealed in God's Word.

God celebrates your choices so much that all of heaven will back your decisions. When you choose to head in a particular direction, God starts sending angels to prepare your way. But the angels do not move until you take the first step."

"I think I understand what you are saying," Zach said, "I recently heard Jesse Duplantis preach. He said that God asks him every morning, 'What are we going to do today, Jesse?' Most of the time, God does not tell him what to do. God allows him to choose, and then God goes along and helps out with his plans. In fact, Jesse Duplantis says he makes 99% of his own decisions."

"Zach, do you ever have trouble making a choice between two different options?" I inquired.

"Oh yeah, I just bought a car and I did not know if God wanted me to get a red car or a blue car."

I recalled that Zach drove a blue car. "How did you choose blue?" I asked.

"Well, I was in the car dealer's lot, and I started to pray. I looked up to heaven and saw the blue sky. I knew it was a sign from God so I bought the blue car," he explained.

"That's an interesting way to decide what color of car to drive," I said, "let me tell you how I would make that decision. If buying the blue car is Option A and buying the red car is Option B, I do not think God would have a preference either way. Sometimes we sit and agonize over whether we should choose Option A or Option B. But, the blessing of God is not on "A" or "B," the blessing is on ME. As long as my decision does not go against God's general will as revealed in the Bible, God will bless no matter which option I choose."

I added, "Although, I would have bought a blue car too. Blue is my favorite color." Then I gave Zach an example from my life, "Recently, our team was trying to decide if God wanted us to do a crusade in a big city in Brazil or in a nearby smaller city. We prayed for guidance, but never heard a definitive word from God. Finally, we decided to do the crusade in the big city because we recognized that God would bless us no matter where we decided to do the crusade. So, when you are wondering if Option A or Option B is better, it is not 'A' or 'B,' it's 'U.' Whatever you decide, God blesses.

Walk in the freedom you have in Christ. God has given us boundaries, but within those boundaries we have great freedom. Even if there is no guarantee of success, move. Be willing to take a risk. Take a step into the unknown. If you do not know what direction to go, just generally align your life to be for what God is for and against what God is against. Just do something; anything that you think would make God happy. If God says 'no' then take a step in another direction. If not, then continue forward and expect God to give you success."

"But I don't want to miss God," Zach protested.

I had an answer. God says, "I'm so big, you can't miss Me! God told us *'Go into all the world and preach the Gospel'* (Mark 16:15). Once we start moving in that direction, He will influence our choice of where to go, but for the most part, He is just happy when we go. It is hard to be out of God's will if you go to the mission field and start telling people about Jesus.

People often wait to be called by God and never go. They say, 'I am waiting to receive my call from God.' In reality, you are already called. As T.L. Osborn says, 'The need is the call.' When you see a need, you are probably the one called to fill that need.

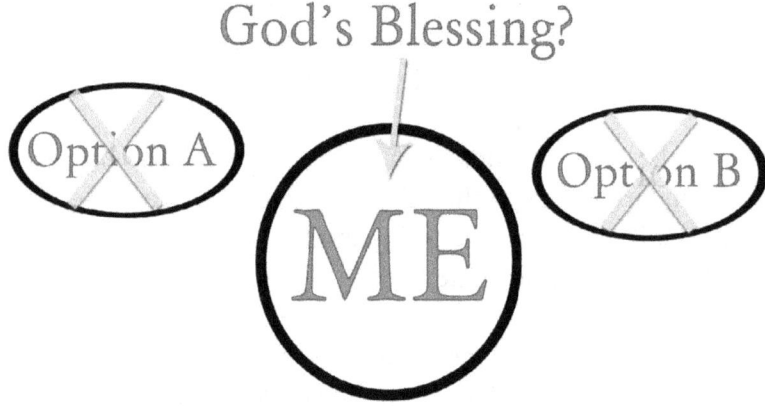

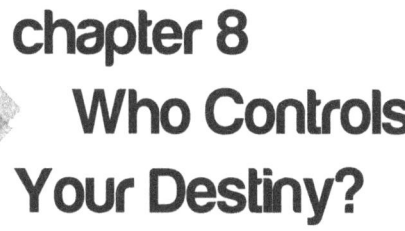

chapter 8
Who Controls Your Destiny?

"Zach," I continued, "who controls what happens here on earth?" I knew it was a trick question, but I wanted Zach to take responsibility for his own choices.

"God," Zach replied.

"God is not in control of what happens here on earth. Bad things frequently occur like hurricanes, tornados, floods, tsunamis, wars, car accidents, and disease. These so-called 'acts of God' are not part of God's nature. God is a good God, yet bad things still happen on earth. This proves that God is not in control. God *'wants all men to be saved'* (1 Timothy 2:4), yet people die unsaved every day. God's will does not always come to pass. The teaching that God is in control is misleading, I think."

Zach thought for a second. "So are you saying Satan is in control of what happens on earth?"

"Absolutely not, Satan is not in control here on earth. There are many people who are saved, healed and delivered every day. If Satan was in control, do you think he would allow anyone to be saved, healed, or set free by the power of

God? If the devil was in control, there would be complete hell on earth."

"Then who controls what happens on the earth?"

"You control what happens to you on this earth. You create your circumstances. God does not control your decisions. God has only predestined the consequences of your decisions. The decisions I make shape my destiny. If I make good decisions, God's will for my life comes to pass. If I make poor decisions, then Satan's will for my life becomes a reality.

The only power that can trump the will of God is the decision of man. The truth is that God's will is seldom done on earth as it is in heaven. Mike Murdock says, 'Your decisions decide your destiny.' Your decisions decide your wealth. Your decisions decide your health. Your decisions decide your relationships. You decide who you marry. You choose where you will live and how much money you will make.

Your life is exactly the way you want it to be. Your choices have brought you to where you are today. If you truly wanted your life to change, it would.

Do you really want your life to be better? There is only one way for that to happen. Take action and move. Notice I didn't say more Bible reading. Or prayer. Or going to church. Or waiting for God to open a door. Or having an anointed preacher lay hands on you. All these things are fine and they can't hurt, but they alone will not change your circumstances. Change can only come when you put action to your decisions.

Your ability to put action to your choices is the most

powerful commodity in the universe. Do not wait around until God decides to bless you, take action so God can bless you. God does not bless your waiting, He blesses your steps. The last five letters of the word 'satisfaction' are action. The Latin word "satis" means "enough." So, enough action produces satisfaction.

Mike Murdock also says, 'Faith decides divine timing.' When you discover the faith to take a step, God begins to move on your behalf.

Many say they have 'faith' but they do not really have faith because they never take action. *'...Faith by itself, if it is not accompanied by action, is dead'* (James 2:17). Action equals movement. We know that faith comes by hearing God's Word (Romans 10:17), but recently God told me that miracles come by doing God's Word.

Faith without action is dead. *'Do not merely listen to the Word, and so deceive yourselves. Do what it says'* (James 1:22). Doing requires moving. We must put what we believe into action in our lives. Many people say they believe God's Word; few actually put God's Word into practice in their daily lives.

Let me give you an example. Your pastor mentions Luke 6:38, *'Give and it will be given to you.'* Everyone cheers, claps their hands, and shouts 'Hallelujah.' Then the offering plate is passed. Instead of putting the verse into action, many keep a death grip on their wallet or purse. Why? Because they say they believe this verse, but they really don't. If they really believed, they would give every time the opportunity presented itself because they know they cannot outgive God.

Your movement reveals what you truly believe.

God has a plan for this world. But His plan is dependent upon humans who have been given free choice. Our choices determine whether or not we participate in His plan. God's plan is set, but the people who implement it are fluid. Your life is part of God's perfect plan. But, God is not the One who makes that plan come to pass in your life. Your choices decide if God's plan will be manifested in your life.

God allows us to make our own decisions. As we make decisions, He walks beside us as a Friend and a Guide. As a Friend, He offers advice. As a Guide, He points us in the right direction. Decisions determine your destiny. The voice of the Holy Spirit shapes and guides our decisions. God's will for your life is revealed as you begin to move."

Zach scratched his head, "So, we have to put action to our faith; and make a decision to do what we know we need to do. Success is not going to happen automatically; we have to make it happen."

I replied, "That's right. Just because God wills something to happen does not mean it will happen; we have to line our will up with God's will. God wants us successful, but we have to say, 'I will be successful.' God wants us to have a good marriage, but we have to say, 'I will have a good marriage.' God wants us to win lots of souls, but we need to say, 'I will win lots of souls.' If you do not will it, it will not happen. The fulfillment of God's will depends on your will.

In the Bible, Joshua learned how to use his will to accomplish God's will. Many times throughout the Book of Joshua, we find him using his will. He says, *'We will do whatever You have commanded us'* (Joshua 1:16); *'We will go wherever You send us'* (Joshua 1:16); *'I will drive out the enemies'* (Joshua 14:12); and *'We will serve the Lord'* (Joshua 24:15,18, 21, 24).

Joshua used his will because he saw firsthand how God used His will. God promised Joshua, *'I will be with you, I will never leave you or forsake you'* (Joshua 1:5).

We will because God will! We use our will to make God's will manifest itself here on earth. Even when you don't feel like doing God's will, use your will to force yourself to move.

Look at the Book of Psalms to see examples of how to use your will, *'I will be glad and rejoice'* (Psalm 9:2); *'I will fulfill my vows'* (Psalm 22:25); *'I will give You thanks forever'* (Psalm 30:12); *'I will perpetuate Your memory through all generations'* (Psalm 45:17); *'I will sing and make music'* (Psalm 57:7); *'I will always have hope; I will praise You more and more'* (Psalm 71:14); *'I will give You thanks…I will exalt You'* (Psalm 118:28).

Your will has been given to you by God as a weapon, as a tool, as a gift. You have to use your will to decide what happens in your life. What will you do?"

Zach thought about my question, but then folded his arms and said stubbornly, "You've built a nice-sounding philosophy, but I am still convinced. I need some Biblical proof. Unless I see two or three witnesses from God's Word, I'm going to throw all your ideas out the window."

"Okay," I said, "I'm preaching at a local church tomorrow on the same truths we have been talking about today. Why don't you come and I will show you a story from the Old Testament where God rewarded a man who was willing to move for his miracle."

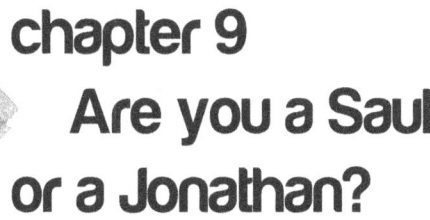

chapter 9
Are you a Saul or a Jonathan?

The next morning, Zach showed up early to church with his Bible in one hand and a notebook in the other. After the song service, the pastor introduced me as the visiting speaker.

I began by talking to the congregation about the differences between sitters and movers. I explained there are two schools of thought concerning God's will. The first school says, "I do not move without God's guidance," the second school of thought says, "I do not expect God's guidance until I move." Sitters wait for God to move. Movers move and expect God to bless their movement.

I asked them to open their Bibles to 1 Samuel 14. Below is a summary of what I shared with the congregation.

In this story, King Saul is an example of a "sitter." The Israelites are hiding in fear from the Philistine army. King Saul was sitting under a pomegranate tree with six hundred men consulting a priest trying to discover God's will. *"Saul was staying on the outskirts of Gibeah under a pomegranate tree in Migron. With him were about six hundred men, among whom was Ahijah, who was wearing an ephod. He was a son of Ichabod's brother Ahitub son of Phinehas, the son of Eli, the LORD's priest in Shiloh"* (1 Samuel 14:2-3).

Meanwhile, King Saul's son Jonathan gives us an example of a "mover." *"On each side of the pass that Jonathan intended to cross to reach the Philistine outpost was a cliff; one was called Bozez, and the other Seneh. One cliff stood to the north toward Micmash, the other to the south toward Geba. Jonathan said to his young armor bearer, 'Come, let's go over to the outpost of those uncircumcised fellows. Perhaps the LORD will act in our behalf. Nothing can hinder the LORD from saving, whether by many or by few'"* (1 Samuel 14:4-6).

Neither Saul or Jonathan knew how God wanted to deliver them. Saul responded the way many Christians respond in this situation. He sat in one place and refused to do anything until he heard from God.

But his son Jonathan responded in a completely different way. He decided to take action. He did not specifically know what God's will was. He said to his armor bearer, "I have a plan. Let's stop hiding and show ourselves to the enemy. Perhaps the Lord will act on our behalf." He did not know if God would move, he just decided to try something in order to see, perhaps, maybe, if God would work in their favor. He started heading in the general direction to attack the Lord's enemies. He followed a compass heading, not a map. He figured that if he went against the enemy God was against, it would give God the opportunity to do a miracle.

Once Jonathan was in motion, he gave God an opportunity to give him a sign. Jonathan said, *"If they say to us, 'Wait there until we come to you,' we will stay where we are and not go up to them. But if they say, 'Come up to us,' we will climb up, because that will be our sign that the LORD has given them into our hands"* (1 Samuel 14:9-10).

What a sign! Jonathan was saying, "We'll come out of hiding, and if the enemy threatens to kill us, then we will know it is a sign from God."

Jonathan's armor bearer was an amazing sidekick. There were only two swords in the whole camp (1 Samuel 13:22). Saul had one sword and Jonathan had the other. Jonathan asked the armor bearer to come along even though he did not have a sword. When you take action, it inspires others to follow. If you do nothing, no one will ever follow you or help you. Reinhard Bonnke says, "Do nothing, and nothing happens; he who does nothing, needs no help."

"So both of them showed themselves to the Philistine outpost. 'Look!' said the Philistines. 'The Hebrews are crawling out of the holes they were hiding in.' The men of the outpost shouted to Jonathan and his armor bearer, 'Come up to us and we'll teach you a lesson.' So Jonathan said to his armor bearer, 'Climb up after me; the LORD has given them into the hand of Israel.' Jonathan climbed up, using his hands and feet, with his armor bearer right behind him. The Philistines fell before Jonathan, and his armor bearer followed and killed behind him. In that first attack Jonathan and his armor bearer killed some twenty men in an area of about half an acre" (1 Samuel 14:11-14).

Jonathan climbs up, attacks the enemy, and kills twenty people. Then, and only then does God start to move. *"Then panic struck the whole army, those in the camp and field, and those in the outposts and raiding parties, and the ground shook.*

It was a panic sent by God" (1 Samuel 14:15). If Jonathan had stayed in hiding with his father, God would never have sent a panic among the enemy. The reason God moved was because Jonathan moved! Jonathan killed twenty enemies before God created a tumult.

Meanwhile, Saul's scouts noticed what was happening. *"Saul's lookouts at Gibeah in Benjamin saw the army melting away in all directions"* (1 Samuel 14:16).

What does King Saul do? Does he join the battle? Does he say, "This is a move of God, let's defeat the enemy?" No. Saul is a "sitter." He continues to sit under the pomegranate tree and again tries to mysteriously discover God's will. *"Saul said to Ahijah, 'Bring the ark of God.'"* (1 Samuel 14:18). Saul was still trying to hear God's voice. Even when God is obviously moving, some Christians still sit around and talk about trying to discover God's will.

Finally, it was so obvious that God was giving them a victory, that Saul said, "Forget about finding out God's will, let's go attack." *"While Saul was talking to the priest, the tumult in the Philistine camp increased more and more. So Saul said to the priest, 'Withdraw your hand.' Then Saul and all his men assembled and went to the battle"* (1 Samuel 14:19-21).

As soon as Saul stopped sitting around and took action, the battle was won. *"They found the Philistines in total confusion, striking each other with their swords. Those Hebrews who had previously been with the Philistines and had gone up with them to their camp went over to the Israelites who were with Saul and Jonathan. When all the Israelites who had hidden in the hill country of Ephraim heard that the Philistines were on the run, they joined the battle in hot pursuit. So the LORD rescued Israel that day, and the battle moved on beyond Beth Aven"* (1 Samuel 14:22-23).

Jonathan did not know what God's plan was. He did not even know if God would do anything but because he took action God honored his movement. Saul was waiting for God to move; Jonathan moved. God provides direction when we start to move.

At the end of the service I gave an altar call, "If you want to be a sitter, stay in your seats. But, if you want to be a mover, stand up and come to the front and let's make a commitment to God that we will never sit still." Everyone in the audience came to the front.

Once you start to move, unless God specifically says "no" then proceed as if it is a "yes."

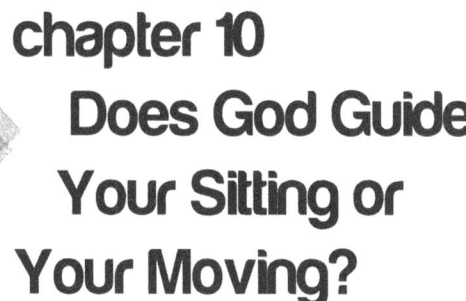

chapter 10
Does God Guide Your Sitting or Your Moving?

That evening I preached at the same church again, but this time I used an example from the New Testament to teach the same lesson.

I read Acts 16:6-10, *"Paul and his companions traveled throughout the region of Phrygia and Galatia, having been kept by the Holy Spirit from preaching the Word in the province of Asia. When they came to the border of Mysia, they tried to enter Bithynia, but the Spirit of Jesus would not allow them to. So they passed by Mysia and went down to Troas. During the night Paul had a vision of a man of Macedonia standing and begging him, 'Come over to Macedonia and help us.' After Paul had seen the vision, we got ready at once to leave for Macedonia, concluding that God had called us to preach the gospel to them."*

Was Paul the Apostle a "sitter" or a "mover?"

Many people have the impression that Paul was so close to God that he never moved without God's specific guidance, but when we examine Paul's life we discover that he was not sitting around waiting to hear God, instead he was actively moving.

In this passage, Paul decided to take his evangelistic team to Asia but the Holy Spirit prevented them from going. Then Paul traveled throughout the region of Phrygia and Galatia until they came to the border of Mysia and tried to enter Bithynia but Jesus did not allow them to enter. Finally, God sent a vision of a man in Macedonia calling for Paul's help.

Notice, Paul did not sit around wondering what God's will was. He did not stay in one place trying to discover if there was something he had done wrong that was preventing him from going to Asia. No. Paul was traveling and ministering. He was taking action. As Paul was moving, God provided direction.

Paul tried to enter Asia; the Holy Spirit said "No." Paul tried to enter Bithynia; Jesus said "No." Finally God the Father put him to sleep so he would stay still long enough to see the vision telling him to go to Macedonia. Paul was so busy moving around; the whole Trinity got involved in guiding him!

Often when people preach about knowing God's will, the vision of the Macedonian man is used as an example of how God guides, but Paul was not just laying around waiting for God to give him a vision. He was actively moving to find a place to preach.

Once Paul was moving, God was able to provide guidance by saying "no." This is guidance by prohibition. Once you start to move, unless God specifically says "no" then proceed as if it is a "yes." God will respond to our movement, even if our movement is in the wrong direction. Always give God the power of veto, but unless He specifically stops you, proceed. Assume a green light unless you are specifically given a red light.

Even when my wife Jessica and I do not have the money or have specific direction from God concerning which city to conduct a Gospel Festival in, we pick a city and start moving in that direction. Sometimes God says "no" through the local pastors who do not feel they want a crusade in their city. Sometimes God says "no" by not providing the money for what we want to do. If this happens we just slightly change our direction. We pick another city or reschedule the event to give us more time to raise money. But we keep moving in the general direction of winning the lost until we find a place of favor.

If we go to city "A" we will be blessed; if we go to city "B" we will be blessed. God is just excited that we are moving. As we move, He directs our steps. But when we stop, God stops speaking until we take another step.

Evangelist Mike Smalley says, "The majority of God's will for your life has already been outlined in the Bible. There is no Scripture that 'commands' us to hear from God on every single decision. It is my personal belief that in many areas of our life, God has 'no will at all.' He simply expects us to make decisions based on the principles of His Word and verified by the peace the Holy Spirit gives us internally. Focus your energies on complete obedience to the 'known will of God' as outlined in the Scripture. As you move forward in obedience, God has promised to direct your specific steps!"

That night after church Zach and I went to a 24-hour pancake restaurant. My wife Jessica joined us for a late night breakfast. After we made some small talk, Zach asked me a follow-up question on one point in my sermon, "Has God ever guided you by saying 'no'?"

"Yes, actually years ago I was dating a young lady. I really liked her a lot, but one day I was praying about our relationship and I distinctly heard God say, 'Daniel, you are not supposed to marry her.' It was difficult, but I broke up with her."

"Do you believe God allows us free choice concerning the person we are supposed to marry? Do you think there is one perfect spouse for me or do you think that there are many different girls I could choose to marry that God would approve of?" I knew these questions were important to Zach because he wanted to get married.

I replied, "A year later, I was interested in another girl. I felt God say, 'She is not My best plan for your life but if you pursue her, she will be yours.' In other words, God gave me permission to have a relationship with her if I wanted to do so, but God did not feel she was the best. She was not outside of God's moral will (I can date whomever I choose as long as she is a believer) but she was outside God's advice. I did not end up marrying her either."

"So how did you finally decide to marry Jessica?"

I smiled at my wife and put my hand on her knee, "When I met Jessica, she fit me and my life calling perfectly and I fit hers. She was already experienced on the mission field. She loved God; she loved people, and she loved me. During our courtship, I only had green lights and confirmations that we were right for each other. I never felt a yellow light or check in my spirit that something was amiss. A year later, I took action and proposed. I know God celebrated my decision to marry Jessica. We ended up being perfect for one another."

Then Jessica shared her testimony of how she ended up on the mission field. "I graduated from a Bible school that taught every believer is called to obey the Great Commission to *'go into all the world and preach the Gospel.'* I was taught that any believer could go to the mission field for a time even without a prophetic word that said 'Thus sayeth the Lord, go' because Jesus commanded all believers to go. When an opportunity came for me to go on a one-year trip to India, I did not feel called to be a missionary. But one night I responded to an altar call for those who were 100% dedicated to doing the will of God.

While I was kneeling at the front of the church, I heard God whisper to me, 'Do you believe in the Great Commission?'

'Of course I do,' I responded. Then I heard Him say, 'Do you believe in the Great Commission enough to go and do something about it?' That night, out of simple obedience to God and His Word, I made a commitment to go to the mission field for one year.

My first few months in India were miserable. I just wanted to finish my twelve months and go home. But I vividly remember the night God called me to be a missionary. I was laying on a thin mattress on a concrete floor in southern India. The electricity had just gone off and the overhead fan no longer moved the hot, humid air in the tiny room. Laying in the darkness, soaking my pillow with sweat, I counted over sixty mosquito bites on my body. God gently spoke to my heart in the darkness, 'Jessica, this is the life I have called you to.'

I did not know whether to laugh or to cry. All I knew was

that God wanted me to work on the mission field for the rest of my life. I felt relieved to finally know my lifetime calling regardless of what it was or the hardships I was bound to face.

The next morning I jumped out of bed and walked to a nearby Internet café to e-mail my headquarters and make a commitment to return to India for a second year. I stepped out onto the mission field with nothing but a simple desire to obey God's Word. But, once I arrived in India, God gave me a clear direction that would last the rest of my life."

After Jessica finished telling her story, we all went home.

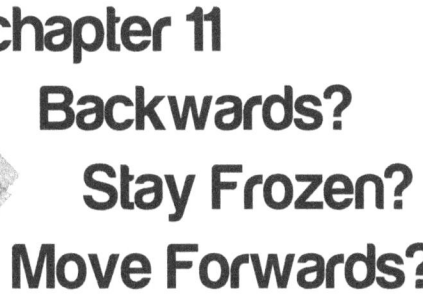

chapter 11
Backwards?
Stay Frozen?
Move Forwards?

The next morning Zach called me and asked for some more Biblical examples. I was happy to oblige.

"Let's look at the Old Testament story of four lepers. The city of Samaria was under attack. The four lepers were sitting outside the gates starving to death. They had a decision to make. Should they go back into the city and go hungry? Should they sit still until they died? Or should they risk visiting the enemy's camp? They faced a question many of us face today. Should we move backwards, stay still, or move forward?

I read 2 Kings 7:3-4, *"The lepers said to each other, 'Why sit we here until we die? If we say, We will enter into the city, then the famine is in the city, and we shall die there: and if we sit still here, we die also. Now therefore come, and let us fall unto the host of the Syrians: if they save us alive, we shall live; and if they kill us, we shall but die.'"*

The four lepers decided to put the principle of movement to work. They stood up and began heading toward the enemy's camp. Their movement allowed God to perform a great miracle, not only for them but for their entire city. Even though there were only four barefoot lepers coming, God caused the enemy army to hear the sound of many chariots, horses, and a great army. They fled. When the lepers arrived in the enemy's camp, they discovered abandoned tents, treasure, and food. Their decision to move saved the city of Samaria!

Because the lepers moved forward, a miracle happened for the entire city. If they had sat still or looked back, the entire population would have starved to death.

Many Christians are paralyzed with indecision. Should I go or should I stay? Should I say 'yes' or 'no?' Should I commit or not? Should I witness to this person or stay silent?

After twenty years as missionaries in Mexico, my mother and father decided to go work in Afghanistan. When they made the committment to go, they had no funding, no place to live, few contacts, and no visas. However, as they took steps toward moving to Afghanistan, all the pieces fell into place. Then suddenly, days before they were supposed to leave, the embassy in Washington denied them a long-term visa. My parents prayed about whether they should stay and wait for a long-term visa or whether they should go with a short-term visa that was only good for thirty days. They chose to go and believe God for a miracle. Sure enough, once they arrived in Afghanistan, God provided a miraculous way for them to get the visas they needed. As they were moving, their miracle arrived.

'How many of you are praying for a friend or family member to get saved?' I often ask church congregations. Almost everyone raises his or her hand. Then I encourage them to pull out their cell phones and call the person they have been praying for. Frequently, the person they call will give his or her life to Jesus over the phone. One man approached me afterward in tears saying, 'I prayed for my uncle for fifteen years and tonight he gave his life to Jesus!' The action of calling and witnessing on the cell phone released the miracle he was praying for.

The success of our ministry is because my wife and I have moved forward in faith and discovered that God was there before us waiting on us to arrive. God is ever faithful.

We just looked at a story in the Old Testament about four lepers. Now, let us look in the New Testament at ten lepers who came to Jesus and pleaded, *'Jesus, have mercy on us.'*

Jesus said to them, *'Go, show yourself to the priests'* (Luke 17:14). Jesus did not heal them immediately. Instead, He asked them to take action to prove their faith.

The Bible says, *'As they went, they were healed.'* As they walked toward the temple to see the priests, their miracle manifested. If they had stayed where they were they might never have been healed. Their miracle was in their movement.

Miracles follow your movement. In Acts 8:5, Philip, the first evangelist, *'went down to the city of Samaria, and preached Christ unto them.'* Notice that he went; he was not sent. God did not tell him to go; he simply went, and then miracles began to happen in that city. If you want to fulfill God's command you have to go. Don't wait to be sent, simply go. We are commanded in Mark 16:15 to *'Go into all the world.'* You do not need to wait until you hear a voice from heaven telling you to go to a particular country, just go and expect God to work there on your behalf."

I was not finished sharing yet, but Zach had to go. We decided to get together again at the coffee shop the next day.

chapter 12
Your Success is Motion-Activated

The next morning, Zach started out with a question, "How does my movement help me succeed?"

I replied, "Last week I was flying through the Chicago airport. I walked into a restroom to wash my hands. After I put soap on my hands, I looked for a handle to turn on the water so I could rinse. But, the faucet had no handle. I waved my hand under the spout and magically water began to pour. The water was motion-activated. In the same way, God is motion-activated. When we move, God begins to pour out His Spirit.

Yesterday my wife sent me to the supermarket to buy some groceries. As I approached the door, the motion detector above the door detected my movement and the door automatically opened. In the same way, movement opens the door of your destiny. Your success is motion-activated. Until you move, doors remain closed, but once you start to move, God opens doors in response to your movement.

Paul gave us a perfect example of this concept. He wrote, *'I went to Troas to preach the gospel of Christ and found that the Lord had opened a door for me'* (2 Corinthians 2:12). Notice, Paul went to Troas, then he found that God had opened a door there. The door was opened by Paul's action of going to Troas."

Zach interjected, "You are saying that God is a God of action. He is a verb, not a noun."

"Exactly!" I said. "When you do something, God will do something. When you take action, He takes action on your behalf. The greatest obstacle to fulfilling God's plan for your life is a lack of movement. If you start moving in the direction you already know you should go, you will begin to see miracles happen. Even if your movement is small, give God something to work with!

We can plan what we are going to do, but once we start moving, God will direct our steps."

I flipped over to another verse, "*'In his heart a man plans his course, but the LORD determines his steps'* (Proverbs 16:9). God wants to direct our movement or steps. God cannot steer a parked car. God will use our movement, even movement in the wrong direction. If you start taking steps, God will guide you into the right direction. Once you begin to move, then God reveals His will for your life step by step.

Your miracle is in your movement! When you start to move, God begins to move on your behalf. Are you waiting on God, or is God waiting on you? Almost any movement should do. Just point your life in the general direction (the compass heading) you think you should be going. Then take a step.

Many churches say they want a New Testament church. What was the distinguishing characteristic of the church in the

Book of Acts? A clue is found in the name of the book! The apostles acted. It is not called the 'Book of Intentions.' Yes, they prayed and waited for the Holy Spirit, but that is only the first chapter. Once they were filled with God's power, they began to move. Zach, you are filled with that same power. If you act, God will move, but if you do not act, God cannot move. Jesus says, 'You are My hands, you are My feet, you are My voice, take Me to the ends of the earth!'"

"But I want to hear God's voice," Zach exclaimed, "I want God to tell me Himself what to do."

I chuckled. "Some people want to hear the thundering roar of God's voice, see a choir of angels, get singed by a burning bush, and receive a note written by the finger of God and delivered by the archangel Gabriel before they move. If you could hear God's voice right now, you would probably hear Him shouting, 'Do something!' If an angel knocked on your door, he might say, 'Do something.'"

Zach got a little angry with me. "I have been praying but I just don't know what country I am supposed to go to. I don't have any money to go. I don't even know anyone in Africa. I have been waiting for God to speak to me, but it seems like the heavens are silent…"

I interrupted him. "Jesus said, *'Go into all the world.'* It does not really matter where you go in the world as a missionary. If you obey Jesus, you will be fulfilling God's will for your life. If you start somewhere, God will direct your steps as you are headed along the way."

"But, I don't even know how to get started in the ministry," he said with despair, "my parents were never in ministry like yours are. It was easy for you to start your ministry. You already knew what to do."

I shook my head. If he only knew the battles I had fought to be in the ministry. But I did not want to discourage him. I replied, "Zach, your ministry does not begin when you arrive on the mission field; it begins with the people in your world. In Matthew 10:8, Jesus commanded His disciples *'As you go, preach...'* It does not say 'when you arrive in Africa, preach.' So, right now you can go to the grocery store and preach, or go to work and preach.

Two-thirds of God's Name is 'Go.' Two-thirds of God's Name backwards is 'Do.' So, if you want to be like God, then 'Go Do.'

The supernatural is when God adds His 'Super' to our 'Natural.' God has already done all the 'Super' He is going to do. Now we must do in the natural what we are supposed to do. God has done His part; now we must do our part, by taking action."

chapter 13
Movement Activates the Power of Prayer

Just then a girl walked up to the table where Zach and I were sitting. I recognized her, but I could not remember her name. She had a bubbly personality, the kind of person everyone enjoys being around.

"Hi Daniel, I just finished reading your book *The Secret of Obed-Edom*. I really liked it!" She continued, "I want to write a book someday."

"Great!" I encouraged her. Then I asked a bunch of questions, "What is the title of your book? Do you know what you want to write about? Have you started writing your book yet? Do you know what you want your cover to look like?" She appeared flustered and did not know how to answer my questions.

Then she fired back her own question, "How did you write your first book?"

"Well, the main thing I did to write my first book was to get started. Then I wrote a few paragraphs every day until it was finished." I encouraged her again, "If you write just a little bit every day, your book will be done before you know it."

"I'll pray about it," she said brightly as she walked away.

I turned back to Zach, "She can pray about writing a book for the rest of her life, but until she cracks open her laptop and starts typing, she will never become an author."

"I guess lots of people are praying about things that would happen if they just started to move," Zach observed.

I told him a joke, "Two fishermen are out on a lake and are suddenly engulfed by a storm. One looks fearfully at the waves and asks, 'Should we row or should we pray?' The other fisherman wisely replies, 'Let's do both.'"

"So, prayer without action is wasted," asked Zach.

"That's right. As Jose Zayas said, 'Action without prayer is arrogance, prayer without action is hypocrisy.' Let me give you four examples of people that have asked me to pray for them," I said, "Let me describe their situations."

"Ashley prays to God for a husband, but she never combs her hair or takes care of her appearance. The Bible says that faith without works is dead. She needs to go out and work it a little bit, I think.

Bob prays daily to God for a job, but fails to send out any resumes or applications.

Jasmine wants to lose weight, but eats a bowl of ice cream after every meal.

Jerry and Christine earnestly pray for a good marriage, but they continually speak negative words to each other.

In these examples, prayer by itself will not get results. For each of them, prayer must be mixed with action in order to obtain results. Joyce Meyer says, 'Some of the things you are praying about, you need to get up and take action on. We are partners with God. He has done His part, now you must do your part.' Peter was not able to walk on the water until he took a step out of the boat. Step out and find out what God wants to do through you.

According to T.L. Osborn, there are two prayers God will never answer. First, when we ask Him to do something He's already done. Second, when we ask Him to do what He told us to do. Dr. Osborn says, 'We pray for God to open the doors of China but God is not going to open the doors of China. We are going to open the doors of China, when we go to China.'

Often when Christians pray they make it sound as if God's holding out on us. As if there is a secret ingredient God has not yet given in order for revival to be possible. We pray, 'God, heal the sick' or 'God, save the lost.' In reality, God has already given us all His power, and done everything He can do to save the lost. He gave His only Son, His very best. What more can God give? What more do you want Him to do for you?"

Since it is so important to take action, I decided to challenge Zach to take a step toward his destiny.

I inquired, "Zach, do you have a passport?"

"Not yet," he replied.

"I firmly believe every believer should own a passport. How can we obey God's command to *'go into all the world,'* unless we have the means of getting there? If God gave you a fully-paid, round-trip ticket to go preach in Africa tomorrow, you would not be able to take advantage of it. Before you can expect God to provide for your mission trip, you must take the first step and get a passport. When you take steps toward your vision, then God begins moving pieces into place for your provision. Years ago, my father and mother heard a preacher say that every believer should own a passport. They applied for passports for our entire family, even us children. Right after the passports arrived, someone paid for our entire family to go to Korea on a ministry trip."

That day I took Zach to get his passport photos. Then we went to the post office, filled out an application, paid a fee, and put it all in the mail to the passport office. Soon, he would have his own ten-year passport.

"I'm so excited!" Zach exclaimed, "It feels good to take action."

chapter 14
A Word from God for Your Life

"Are you excited about your passport coming?" I asked the next time I saw Zach.

"Absolutely! I feel like I have had a major breakthrough on my dream of becoming a missionary," Zach replied.

"You are definitely on your way!"

Zach was still bothered, "I know God wants me to be a missionary, but I guess one of the things that has held me back is that I have been waiting for God to speak to me about every step of the process of getting to the mission field."

I said, "I know many people who face a similar problem. The reason a lot of believers don't move is because they have not received a specific word from God about moving. They pretend to be so dependent on God that they never get anything done without Him. I know one person who wakes up in the morning and actually asks God if he should brush his teeth."

Zach pretended to speak in a deep baritone imitation of God's voice, "Thou shalt not have bad breath today."

I laughed. "You don't need God's help to make every little decision. He will give you guidance on your big life goals but He often trusts you enough to let you make the daily choices about your life."

"But, does God give us explicit instructions sometimes?"

"Absolutely. It is true that God will speak to you and give you detailed, urgent instructions from time to time. When He does, you should promptly obey. One of my friends was about to get on an airplane. God spoke to him, 'Don't get on that plane.' My friend did not want to miss his flight, but he obeyed God and changed his flight. Later while watching the news he found out the plane had crashed. Think how relieved he was to have heard and obeyed God's voice! However, in my life most of the instructions God has given me are the type of tasks that take years to complete."

"What do you mean?"

"Let me tell you a story about a word I received from God. Three months before I started college, God spoke to me several times, and in several different ways. Each time He spoke, He said exactly the same thing.

The first time God gave me this message, I heard His voice inside my spirit. I was reading the Bible and I came across the verse, *'The soul of the diligent shall be made rich'* (Proverbs 13:4). I heard God speak to my spirit, 'Daniel, be diligent.'

A few days later, I was eating lunch with John & Shirley

Tasch. They are the former children's pastors at the church where I grew up. Pastor John told me, 'Daniel, God says that if you will be diligent, you will be successful.'

Later that same week, Pastor Billy Allen from Christ for the Nations Church gave me almost exactly the same word from God, 'Daniel, you will be successful if you are diligent.'

Then, my parents prayed over me as I left home for college and told me once again, 'Daniel, be diligent.' Since I had heard this message from so many confirming voices in a short period of time, I knew it was a word from God. I found it in the Bible, heard it from God Himself, and it was reaffirmed by several trusted mentors.

I remember being very excited about receiving this word from God. I thought it was an instruction from God designed to help me for the first few months of college. I figured that after a few months of being diligent, God would give me another word to help me with the next stage in my life.

However, several months went by and I did not hear any follow-up word from God. So, I continued being diligent. I studied hard for my tests. I was industrious. I continually looked for opportunities to minister to people. And I waited to hear more from God. But no further instruction came.

During all four years of college, this same word from God continued to sustain me. I graduated with a 4.0 grade point average. My senior paper was chosen as the best in my field of study. I graduated from Oral Roberts University with honors, all because of obedience to God's word for my life.

Over time, I realized that this word about being diligent applies to the rest of my life. To this day I continue to be diligent in my life and ministry. I did not need dozens of different instructions from God. All I needed was to take action on the one instruction I received.

I am still being diligent. The word I thought was for a season turned out to be for the rest of my life. You do not need lots of different words from God; all you need is to be obedient and to walk out the commands you have already received."

Zach thought about my story. "Do you know of anyone else who took years to complete one of God's instructions?"

"I heard Oral Roberts say that he had heard the audible voice of God only a handful of times in his entire life. On one word from God, Oral built a nation wide healing ministry; on another he built the premier charismatic university in the world. Every major instruction God gave him took a decade or more to complete.

Another example is my pastor, Billy Joe Daugherty. He was driving down the street one day and God gave him a vision of the church building he would one day build. He stopped and drew a sketch of what he had seen. It took twenty years before the vision came to pass, but eventually the vision was fulfilled in every detail.

In Genesis, Joseph had a dream of his brothers bowing before him. It took more than thirty years for the dream to come true. Even though the dream took a long time, and Joseph went through many hardships, he remained faithful to God, trusting that eventually the dream would come to pass."

Zach asked, "But what if God has never given me a big word for my life? You received a prophecy as a child that you are called to be an evangelist. I have never received a word like that from God."

I replied, "Every person is going to have a different experience. God works with each of us according to our unique personality and individual need. Just continue to take steps toward what you already know to do and as you move, God will direct your steps. The closer you get to your destination, the more clear your destiny will become."

God is so big that you can't miss Him.

chapter 15
Are You Waiting on God or is God Waiting on You?

I was out of town preaching in different parts of the country for several weeks, so Zach and I continued our conversation by telephone.

"Hey Daniel, I've been thinking about what you have been saying to me."

"Did you learn anything? How are you going to be successful in life?" I asked.

"I'm trusting God," he replied.

"God is trusting you!" I said.

"But I have faith."

I answered, "Faith without works is dead. You need to work a little bit. You have to put your faith into action."

"What if I miss God?"

"God is so big that you can't miss Him. If you miss God, don't worry, He will find you."

"I'm waiting for God," Zach explained.

"No! God is waiting for you," I fired back.

"I am praying for an open door."

"How can you expect God to open a door unless you are knocking?"

" I don't know for sure if God has called me."

"The need is the call. If you see a need, you are probably called to fill it."

"But, I don't want to run ahead of God," he protested.

"Do you really think you can? God is fast! The God who created the universe is not just behind us, He is before us."

"What if I go in the wrong direction?" Zach asked.

"God will guide your steps back to the right path."

"But, what if I fall?"

I suddenly realized that he was just messing with me. "God will catch you!" I exclaimed.

"Daniel, I think I am beginning to get it! We should put together a list of questions to help people discover God's will for their lives. I think that would really help people."

"I think that's a great idea. Let's work on it when I return."

"Good. Talk to you later," Zach said.

"Bye," I said as I hung up.

Satan usually shouts;
the Holy Spirit often whispers.

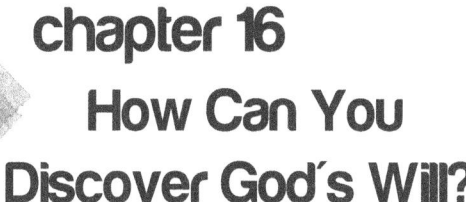

chapter 16
How Can You Discover God's Will?

When I returned home from traveling, Zach and I met for dinner at my house. My wife Jessica joined in on the conversation as we consumed chicken quesadillas with hot salsa.

"Zach, explain to Jessica what you want us to do," I began.

"Well, I have had difficulty knowing what God's will is in different situations. I am sure a lot of other people are in the same situation. We were thinking that we could put together a list of questions that would help people discover God's will for their lives."

Jessica grabbed a piece of paper and a pen to help us keep track of the questions. At the top of the page she scribbled, **"What does the Bible say about what I want to do?"**

I glanced at what she had written. "That's right. The Bible reveals God's moral will for your life. If it is against God's will as revealed in the Bible, then it is against His will for your life."

"Sometimes God does tell us exactly what to do," Zach said. "Write down **'Has God given me specific instructions concerning this decision?'** Remember, Oral Roberts built a university because God specifically told him, 'Build me an university.'"

I added a story about my father, "Many years ago, God spoke to my father, 'Move to El Paso, Texas, and establish your headquarters at Rancho Del Rey.' In obedience to this specific instruction, our family moved to El Paso. My father started looking for land to buy. One day, he saw a huge billboard that said, "Rancho Del Rey." It was literally a sign from God. Miraculously, we were able to use that land as a missions base for over twenty years.

One thing that helps me know if I am in God's will is a sense of peace," Jessica said as she wrote, **'Do I have peace about this decision?'** "One of my favorite verses is Colossians 3:12, *'Let the peace of God rule in your hearts.'* God often leads through a sense of peace. Sometimes God's direction is dramatic, like when He opened up the Red Sea for the Israelites to escape the Egyptians. But, dramatic revelation will not always reveal the way God wants you to go. Most of the time, God intervenes in our lives in a quieter fashion. Elijah looked for God in the wind and the fire, but instead God spoke with a still, small voice."

Jessica added another thought, "Satan usually shouts, the Holy Spirit often whispers. I never want to do anything that I do not feel peace about. We should always ask, **"What is the voice of the Holy Spirit saying?"** She quoted a verse from memory, *"But when He, the Spirit of truth, comes, He will guide you into all truth"* (John 16:13 NIV).

"It is important to ask the advice of wise spiritual advisors," I said, "Proverbs 11:14 reads, *'For lack of guidance a nation falls, but many advisers make victory sure.'* It is always easier to learn from the mistakes of others than it is to learn from your own mistakes. Jessica, write down, **'What do my mentors say about this decision?'"**

Zach spoke up, "Perhaps you should ask **'Will this harm me physically or mentally?'** 1 Corinthians 6:19 says your body is the temple of the Holy Ghost so you should never do anything that is likely to harm you. This might help you decide whether you should go skydiving or eat a third piece of pie or go to a horror movie."

"I remember a question one of my professors often asked, **'Will this help me love God and others more?'"** I added, "Another good question, **'Will this course of action bring me closer to Jesus?'"**

Jessica came up with another query, **"'Will this help me lead a holy life?'** 1 Peter 1:16 says, *'Be holy, because I am holy.'* In everything we do, we should ask, **'Will this glorify God?'** 1 Corinthians 10:31 reads, *'So whether you eat or drink or whatever you do, do it all for the glory of God.'"*

"What about putting out a fleece like Gideon did in Judges 6?" Zach asked, "Remember, Gideon asked God to confirm His instructions by leaving a fleece out on a dew-soaked lawn. He asked God to make the fleece wet and the lawn dry. The next day he asked God to make the lawn wet and the fleece dry."

"I've heard of people using fleeces," Jessica shared, "I have one friend who was trying to discover God's will. She closed her eyes and opened her Bible to a random spot, then put her finger down on the page. The verse she was pointing at directly answered her question."

I remembered a joke, "A man was facing a big problem and decided to see what instruction he could find in his Bible. He closed his eyes, flipped open his Bible and stabbed his finger down. The verse he was pointing at said, 'Judas went and hanged himself.' He thought, 'That can't be what God wants me to do.' So he decided to try again. This time the verse he pointed to read, 'Go thou and do likewise.' Obviously, God did not want him to commit suicide."

Jessica laughed. She usually does not think my jokes are funny, but she sometimes laughs anyways, less at my jokes and more at my silliness. Jessica replied, "I think that sometimes God honors the requests of people who put out fleeces to test His will, but for the most part, I think that putting out fleeces is something that an immature believer does. Mature believers simply follow God's revealed will and make good choices."

"We could just flip a coin," Zach joked.

"That's true. In the Old Testament the priests used to cast lots, basically the equivalent of rolling dice, to determine God's will. But I think that most of the time, there are much better ways of discovering God's will. Rather then testing God with a fleece, I think you should ask, **'Is this a wise choice?'** I flipped open my Bible and read two verses about wisdom. *"Be very careful, then, how you live, not as unwise but as wise, making the most of every opportunity, because the days* *are evil. Therefore do not be foolish, but understand what the Lord's will is"* (Ephesians 5:15-17 NIV). *"If any of you lacks wisdom, he should ask God, who gives generously to all without finding fault, and it will be given to him"* (James 1:5 NIV).

Jessica went into the kitchen to refill our glasses with juice from the refrigerator. Zach said, "Often, the simplest solution to a problem is the best. We should ask, **'Is this the most logical, effective, sensible thing to do?'"**

"That's right!" I exclaimed, "God gave us brains and He expects us to use them. But remember, the world's wisdom is different than God's wisdom." I found Romans 12:2, *"Do not conform any longer to the pattern of this world, but be transformed by the renewing of your mind. Then you will be able to test and approve what God's will is, his good, pleasing and perfect will."*

"Is this God's perfect timing?" Jessica interjected from the kitchen, "When we ask God a question, He may say 'yes,' 'no,' or 'wait.' All three are answers to our questions. Sometimes God wants us to wait for better timing. The Psalmist said, *'Wait for the LORD; be strong and take heart and wait for the LORD'* (Psalm 27:14 NIV). Delay is not a denial. God's not late; perhaps you are early."

I added, "Another great question is, **'Will this enslave me or prevent me from fulfilling God's plan for my life?'** Paul said, *'Everything is permissible for me, but not everything is beneficial. Everything is permissible for me, but I will not be mastered by anything'* (1 Corinthians 6:12 NIV). Paul realized that while God allows us many options, not every option is optimal. Let me give you an example. Zach, you want to go minister on the mission field, don't you?"

"That's right."

"You could go buy a house tomorrow. It would not necessarily be out of God's will for you to buy a house, but if you had high monthly payments, the debt on a house could become a chain that would keep you from your destiny."

Zach said, "I think I see what you are saying. It would be permissible for me to buy a house, but it may not be beneficial at this time. Or if I decided to marry a girl who never wanted to go to the mission field, but wanted me to have a stable job close to home, I would have to choose between the marriage and my calling."

Jessica provided the final question, **"Will this decision help fulfill the Great Commission?"** She spoke for both of us. "As missionary evangelists, we feel that Jesus' command to *'go into all the world'* is one of our most important priorities. So many people get caught up in the hustle and bustle of everyday living, they forget the great assignment God has given us during our time here on earth."

Jessica turned her paper around and showed us the whole list.

1. What does the Bible say about what I want to do?
2. Has God given me specific instructions concerning this decision?
3. Do I have peace about this decision?
4. What is the voice of the Holy Spirit saying?
5. What do my mentors say about this decision?
6. Will this harm me physically or mentally?
7. Will this help me love God and others more?
8. Will this course of action bring me closer to Jesus?
9. Will this help me lead a holy life?
10. Will this glorify God?
11. Is this a wise choice?
12. Is this the most logical, effective, sensible thing to do?
13. Is this God's perfect timing?
14. Will this enslave me or prevent me from fulfilling God's plan for my life?
15. Will this decision help fulfill the Great Commission?

**Don't sit on your butt asking "what?"
Get up and do something new.**

chapter 17
What Steps are You Taking to Fulfill Your Destiny?

I was out of town for over a month for a series of gospel festivals in Asia. When I returned, Zach and I met again.

Zach greeted me with a great big smile, "Guess what, Daniel? I decided to make a commitment to go as a missionary to the nation of Congo. I will be there at least one year."

"Good for you!" I was excited.

"Instead of waiting for God to provide the money, I wrote a letter to thirty of my friends and family members explaining what I am going to do. To my surprise, my great-uncle, who I have never even met, gave me enough money to buy my plane ticket. Some of my other friends promised to support me monthly so I should have enough to survive while I am over there for the year."

"Did you get your airline ticket?" I asked.

Zach replied, "I sure did. I leave in one month. It is a good thing you encouraged me to get a passport when you did, otherwise the timing would not have worked out. I have sold my car, gotten completely out of debt, and the current lease on my apartment is finished in a couple of weeks."

"Awesome!" I exclaimed.

"Daniel, our talks radically changed the way I want to approach life. Instead of sitting around asking God 'What should I do?' I have decided to get up and move toward fulfilling my destiny. In fact, I took all the wisdom we learned in our talks and condensed it to one sentence."

"And what is that sentence?" I asked curiously.

Zach would not tell me right away. "I liked my new motto so much that I printed it out and hung it up on my bathroom mirror so I can see it every day."

"And your motto is…"

Zach replied with a grin, "Don't sit on your butt asking 'what?' Get up and do something new."

I winced in mock pain. "I'm not sure that's how I would put it."

"But seriously," Zach continued, "I am so excited. I'm going to do something big for God."

"Let me pray for you as you launch out on this new adventure."

"Okay."

"Dear God in heaven, I know You are with Zach as he

goes to Africa. Thank You for providing for him. I pray that as he takes these steps toward his destiny, he will be sensitive to Your voice and follow Your leading. I know that as he steps out in faith, You will guide his steps. Thank You for leading him as he fulfills Your will for his life. In Jesus' Name, Amen."

"Amen."

God's plan for your life will never come to pass unless you begin moving.

Epilogue

I pray that Zach's story will inspire you to move forward toward fulfilling God's will for your life. He was called by God to be a missionary and when he started taking steps in that direction, God began to open doors for him. You may not be called to be a missionary, but there is something you can do for God.

God has a great plan for you life. However, God's plan for your life will never come to pass unless you begin moving. As you begin to take steps in the direction of your destiny, God is going to do some amazing miracles for you!

It is time to stop sitting still. Time is short. We need to make every second count for God! There is a world full of people who need Jesus.

God is counting on you to make a difference in this world.

I look forward to hearing about what you accomplish for God's kingdom as you take a step of faith and begin to move.

Always moving,

Daniel King

Our Goal?
Every Soul!

Daniel & Jessica King

About the Author

Daniel King and his wife Jessica met in the middle of Africa while they were both on a mission trip. They are in high demand as speakers at churches and conferences all over North America. Their passion, energy, and enthusiasm are enjoyed by audiences everywhere they go.

They are international missionary evangelists who do massive soul-winning festivals in countries around the world. Their passion for the lost has taken them to over fifty nations preaching the gospel to crowds that often exceed 50,000 people.

Daniel was called into the ministry when he was five years old and began to preach when he was six. His parents became missionaries to Mexico when he was ten. When he was fourteen he started a children's ministry that gave him the opportunity to minister in some of America's largest churches while still a teenager.

At the age of fifteen, Daniel read a book where the author encouraged young people to set a goal to earn $1,000,000. Daniel reinterpreted the message and determined to win 1,000,000 people to Christ every year.

Daniel has authored ten books including his best sellers *Healing Power*, *The Secret of Obed-Edom*, and *Fire Power*. His book *Welcome to the Kingdom* has been given away to tens of thousands of new believers.

Soul Winning Festivals

When Daniel King was fifteen years old, he set a goal to lead 1,000,000 people to Jesus before his 30th birthday. Instead of trying to become a millionaire, he decided to lead a million "heirs" into the kingdom of God. *"If you belong to Christ then you are heirs"* (Galatians 3:29).

After celebrating the completion of this goal, Daniel & Jessica made it their mission to go for one million souls every year.

This **Quest for Souls** is accomplished through:
* Soul Winning Festivals
* Leadership Training
* Literature Distribution
* Humanitarian Relief

Would you help us lead
people to Jesus by joining
The MillionHeir's Club?

Visit www.kingministries.com to get involved!

GET THE LATEST

THE SECRET OF OBED-EDOM

Unlock the secret to supernatural promotion and a more intimate walk with God. Unleash amazing blessing in your life!

$20.00

MOVE

What is God's will for your life? Learn how to find and fulfill your destiny.

$10.00

POWER OF FASTING

Discover deeper intimacy with God and unleash the answer to your prayers.

$10.00

TOLL FREE: 1-877-431-4276
PO Box 70113
TULSA, OK 74170 USA

ORDER ONLINE
WWW.KINGMINISTRIES.COM

THE POWER SERIES

HEALING POWER

Do you need healing? This power-packed book contains 17 truths to activating your healing today!

(BK 02) $20.00

FIRE POWER

Inside these pages you will learn how to CATCH the fire of God, KEEP the fire of God, and SPREAD the fire of God!

(BK 01) $12.00

POWER OF THE SEED

Discover the power of Seedtime & Harvest! Discover why your giving is the most important thing you will ever do!

(BK 04) $20.00

Toll Free: 1-877-431-4276
PO Box 701113
Tulsa, OK 74170 USA

Order Online:
WWW.KingMinistries.com

The Soul Winning Series

Master Soul Winner

Learn practical tips on sharing your faith with friends and family.

$10.00

Soul Winning

Do you have a passion for the lost? This book shares over 150 truths about soul winning.

$10.00

Welcome to the Kingdom

This is a perfect book for new believers. Learn how to be saved, healed, and delivered.(Available in bulk discounts)

$10.00

Toll Free: 1-877-431-4276
PO Box 701113
Tulsa, OK 74170 USA

Order Online:
www.KingMinistries.com

The vision of King Ministries is to lead 1,000,000 people to Jesus every year and to train believers to become leaders.

To contact Daniel & Jessica King:

Write:
King Ministries International
PO Box 701113
Tulsa, OK 74170 USA

King Ministries Canada
PO Box 3401
Morinville, Alberta T8R 1S3 Canada

Call toll-free:
1-877-431-4276

Visit us online:
www.kingministries.com

E-Mail:
daniel@kingministries.com

www.ingramcontent.com/pod-product-compliance
Lightning Source LLC
Chambersburg PA
CBHW071725040426
42446CB00011B/2228